A Service of the Word

and

Affirmations of Faith

Authorized for use in the Church of England

CHURCH HOUSE PUBLISHING
Church House, Great Smith Street, London SW1P 3NZ

ISBN 0 7151 3757 3

Published 1994 for the General Synod of the Church of England
by Church House Publishing

AUTHORIZATION

A Service of the Word and *Affirmations of Faith* are authorized pursuant
to Canon B 2 of the Canons of the Church of England for use from
10 November 1993 to 31 December 2000.

Decisions as to which of the authorized services are to be used (other than
occasional offices) shall be taken jointly by the incumbent and the parochial
church council.

COPYRIGHT

A Service of the Word

INTRODUCTION

A SERVICE OF THE WORD is unusual for an authorized Church of England service. It consists almost entirely of notes and directions and allows for considerable local variation and choice within a common structure. It is important that those who prepare for and take part in *A Service of the Word* should have a clear understanding of the nature of worship and of how the component parts of this service work together. Leading people in worship is leading people into mystery, into the unknown and yet the familiar. This spiritual activity is much more than getting the words or the sections in the right order. The primary object in the careful planning and leading of the service is the spiritual direction which enables the whole congregation to come into the presence of God to give him glory. Choices must be made responsibly by leaders of this service or by groups planning worship with them, whether the service is an occasional one, or a regular one which might use a service card. The notes and the text of *A Service of the Word* should be read together as they interpret one another.

MINISTRY OF THE WORD

At the heart of the service is *The Ministry of the Word*. This must not be so lightly treated as to appear insignificant compared with other parts of the service. The Readings from Holy Scripture are central to this part, and, together with the season, may determine the theme of the rest of the worship. At certain times of the year, as Note 5 says, the readings come from an authorized lectionary, so that the whole Church is together proclaiming the major events in the Christian story. Telling that story and expounding it in the 'sermon' can be done in many different and adventurous ways. Some are suggested in Notes 5 and 7, but there are many others. The word 'sermon' is used in the service, and explained in the note, precisely because it would be too limiting to use words like 'address', 'talk', 'instruction', 'meditation'. The items in sections 5 to 8 may come in any order, and more than once. So the sermon may be in parts, and there may be more than one psalm or song, and of course hymns may be inserted as well. But on most occasions it will be appropriate for this part of the service to have a creed or affirmation of faith as its climax.

PREPARATION

With the Ministry of the Word becoming clear it will be easier to see how *The Preparation* for it, and the response to it in *The Prayers* fit in. People need to know when the service has started (Note 1). What happens at the beginning can create an atmosphere for worship and set the tone and mood for what follows. The gathering of the congregation and the call to worship are to be marked by a liturgical Greeting between minister and people. Leaders should have worked out exactly where this comes among the singing, Scripture sentence, introduction (perhaps to the theme), and opening prayer. All these should draw the members of the congregation together and focus their attention on almighty God.

This part of the service will usually include the Prayers of Penitence, though these may come later if, for instance, the theme of the Ministry of the Word appropriately leads to penitence. Authorized Prayers of Penitence include all those confessions and absolutions in the Book of Common Prayer and the Alternative Service Book, together with several other seasonal and thematic forms, mostly for occasional use, which are set out for convenience in Appendix 1. The climax of this part of the service is either the collect or, if that is included in the prayers, one of the items of praise in section 3. The collect does not have to be that of the day; it may be a thematic one based on the readings (in which case it should be at section 4), or be used to sum up the prayers (in section 9).

PRAYERS

Part of the response to the Word is the Creed, but the response should be developed in *The Prayers* which follow. There are many different options for this part of the service. These range from a series of collect-type prayers to congregational involvement in prayer groups, visual and processional prayers, with responsive forms and a number of people sharing the leading of intercessions in between. But, whatever the form, it is essential that *The Prayers* also includes thanksgiving. A section of thanksgiving, which may include the spoken word, music and hymns, may be the proper climax to this part of the service.

CONCLUSION

Many different words have been used for *The Conclusion*, each of which has something to contribute to our understanding of how the service ends: dismissal, farewell, goodbye, departure, valediction, commission, blessing, ending, going out . . . What is essential, as with the way the service starts, is that it should have a clear liturgical ending: options are listed in Note 9.

Once the service is planned, leaders will want to check through to ensure there is the right balance between the elements of word, prayer and praise, and between congregational activity and congregational passivity. Does the music come in the right places? Is there sufficient silence (Note 4)? This is something leaders can be afraid of, or fail to introduce properly. And is there a clear overall direction to the service: is it achieving the purpose of bringing the congregation together to give glory to God?

A SERVICE OF THE WORD

In this form of service, the material is described as 'authorized' or 'suitable', which expressions shall have the following meanings:

'authorized' means approved by General Synod in accordance with the provisions of Canon B2.

'suitable' means a form used at the discretion of the minister conducting the form of service on any occasion, but such that the material so used shall be neither contrary to, nor indicative of any departure from, the doctrine of the Church of England in any essential matter.

This service is authorized as an alternative to Morning Prayer and Evening Prayer. It is not intended for daily prayer, but to provide a structure for Sunday services and weekday services of an occasional nature.

NOTES

1 **Liturgical Greeting** (section 1)
The service shall have *a clear beginning*. The liturgical Greeting may follow some introductory singing, or a hymn or a sentence of Scripture, and may be followed by a brief introduction or an opening prayer.

2 **Penitence** (section 2)
Authorized Prayers of Penitence includes those forms of confession and absolution in the Appendix. The minister introduces the confession with suitable words.

3 **Hymns, Canticles, Acclamations, and The Peace** (section 3)
Points are indicated for some of these, but if occasion requires they may occur elsewhere.

4 **Silence**
Periods of silence may be kept at different points of the service. It may be particularly appropriate in sections 1, 2, 5 and 9.

5 **Readings** (section 5)
There should preferably be at least *two readings from Holy Scripture*, but it is recognized that if occasion demands there may only be one reading. They may be dramatized, sung or read responsively. The readings shall come from an authorized lectionary during the periods from Advent 3 to Epiphany 1 and from Palm Sunday to Trinity Sunday and whenever the service is combined with the Eucharist.

6 **Psalms** (section 6)
The service shall normally include *a psalm or psalms*. These might be said or sung in the traditional way, but it is also possible to use a metrical version, a responsive form or a paraphrase such as can be found in many current hymnbooks. The psalm may occasionally be replaced by a song or canticle the words of which are taken directly from Scripture, a 'scriptural song'.

7 **Sermon** (section 7)
The term *sermon* may include less formal exposition, the use of drama, interviews, discussion, and audio-visuals. Hymns or other sections of the service may be inserted between parts of the sermon. The sermon may come after one of the readings, or before or after the prayers.

8 **Sermon and Creed** (sections 7 and 8)
The sermon and a creed or authorized *Affirmation of Faith* may be omitted except on *Sundays and Principal Holy Days*.

9 **Conclusion** (section 11)
The service shall have a *clear ending*. This shall include one or more of the following forms: the Peace, the Grace, or a suitable ascription or blessing. If a responsive conclusion (such as the Dismissal at section 55 in ASB Rite A) is used, it shall come last.

THE PREPARATION

1 The minister welcomes the people with a **liturgical Greeting**.

2 **Authorized Prayers of Penitence** are used here or in THE PRAYERS.

3 *Venite, Kyries, Gloria,* a hymn, song, or a set of responses may be used.

4 **The Collect** is said either here or at section 9.

THE MINISTRY OF THE WORD

This includes

5 **Readings (or a Reading) from Holy Scripture**

6 **A psalm**, or, if occasion demands, a scriptural song

7 **A sermon**

8 **An authorized creed**, or, if occasion demands, an authorized **Affirmation of Faith**

THE PRAYERS

These include

9 **Intercessions and thanksgivings**

10 **The Lord's Prayer**

THE CONCLUSION

11 The service concludes with a **liturgical ending.**

Page 71 of *The Alternative Service Book 1980* is amended as follows to include A Service of the Word.

Morning Prayer or Evening Prayer or A Service of the Word with Holy Communion Rite A

47

	MP	EP
Penitence	1-7 optional	24-30
Versicles	8	31
Psalms	9, 10	32, 33
1st Reading	11	34
Canticle	12 optional	35 optional
2nd Reading	13	36
Canticle	15	38
Apostles' Creed	16	39 optional
Collect of the day	20	43
Daily Collect(s)	21 optional, 22	44 optional, 45

	A Service of the Word
Greeting	1
Penitence	2 optional
Canticles etc.	3 optional
Collect	4
Reading(s)	5
Psalm	6
Gospel	5
Sermon	7
Creed	8

	HC
General Intercession or Prayer for the Church and World	20, 21, 81
Penitence (if not used above)	23-29, 80
The Peace	30-31
The Preparation of the Gifts	32-35
The Eucharistic Prayer	36-41
The Communion	42-49, 66, 85
After Communion	50-56, 77, 86

The Shorter Form of Evening Prayer is not suitable for combination with Holy Communion.

References to Morning Prayer and Evening Prayer on pages 239, 251, and 260 of the ASB shall also be taken as referring to A Service of the Word.

AUTHORIZED FORMS OF CONFESSION AND ABSOLUTION

One of the forms in the ASB should normally be used. It may sometimes be helpful to vary the form on particular occasions, in which case a Confession and an Absolution from this authorized list should be used. If possible, an Absolution should be chosen which reflects the style, in language and length, of the Confession. 'Us' and 'our' are said by those who are not ordained priest: words in italics indicate the points where changes may be necessary.

1   CONFESSIONS

I   KYRIE

Notwithstanding any other provision made in ASB 1980, short
sentences may be inserted between the petitions of the Kyrie,
suitable for particular seasons or themes. The insertion of such
sentences may replace any form of confession, provided that the
sentences are of a penitential character and are followed by an
authorized form of absolution.

II   OTHER PENITENTIAL MATERIAL

The forms of confession in the Order of Holy Communion and
Morning and Evening Prayer in the Book of Common Prayer may
be used on any occasion.

1   *Incarnation*

Christ the Light of the World has come to dispel the darkness
of our hearts. In his light let us examine ourselves and
confess our sins.

Silence is kept.

Lord of grace and truth,

we confess our unworthiness
to stand in your presence as your children.

We have sinned:
Forgive and heal us.

The Virgin Mary accepted your call
to be the mother of Jesus.
Forgive our disobedience to your will.

We have sinned:
Forgive and heal us.

Your Son our Saviour
was born in poverty in a manger.
Forgive our greed and rejection of your ways.

We have sinned:
Forgive and heal us.

The shepherds left their flocks
to go to Bethlehem.
Forgive our self-interest and lack of vision.

We have sinned:
Forgive and heal us.

The wise men followed the star
to find Jesus the King.
Forgive our reluctance to seek you.

We have sinned:
Forgive and heal us.

2   *Lent, Penitence*

Let us admit to God the sin which always confronts us.

Lord God,
we have sinned against you;
we have done evil in your sight.
We are sorry and repent.
Have mercy on us according to your love.
Wash away our wrong-doing and cleanse us from our sin.
Renew a right spirit within us
and restore us to the joy of your salvation,
through Jesus Christ our Lord. Amen.   *Psalm 51*

3   *Cross, failure in discipleship*

Lord Jesus Christ,
we confess we have failed you as did your first disciples.
We ask for your mercy and your help.

Our selfishness betrays you:
Lord, forgive:
Christ have mercy

We fail to share the pain of your suffering:
Lord, forgive:
Christ have mercy

We run away from those who abuse you:
Lord, forgive:
Christ have mercy

We are afraid of being known to belong to you:
Lord, forgive:
Christ have mercy   *CFW no. 220 adapted* [2]

4   *Resurrection, Heaven, Glory, Transfiguration, Death,*
         Funerals

O Jesus Christ, risen master and triumphant Lord,
we come to you in sorrow for our sins,
and confess to you our weakness and unbelief:

We have lived by our own strength,
and not by the power of your resurrection.
In your mercy, forgive us:
Lord, hear us and help us.

We have lived by the light of our own eyes,
as faithless and not believing.
In your mercy, forgive us:
Lord, hear us and help us.

We have lived for this world alone,
and doubted our home in heaven.
In your mercy, forgive us:
Lord, hear us and help us.   *CFW no. 244* [2]

5   *Trinity, Mission*

O King enthroned on high,
filling the earth with your glory:
holy is your name,
Lord God almighty.
In our sinfulness we cry to you
to take our guilt away,
and to cleanse our lips to speak your word,
through Jesus Christ our Lord. **Amen.**

                         CFW no. 330 adapted [2]

---

[2] Numbers in right-hand margin refer to Acknowledgements (page 32)

6   *Creation, Harvest*

We confess our sin, and the sin of our society,
in the misuse of God's creation:

God our Father, we are sorry
for the times when we have used your gifts carelessly,
and acted ungratefully.
Hear our prayer, and in your mercy:
forgive us and help us.

We enjoy the fruits of the harvest,
but sometimes forget that you have given them to us.
Father, in your mercy:
forgive us and help us.

We belong to a people who are full and satisfied,
but ignore the cry of the hungry.
Father, in your mercy:
forgive us and help us.

We are thoughtless,
and do not care enough for the world you have made.
Father, in your mercy:
forgive us and help us.

We store up goods for ourselves alone,
as if there were no God and no heaven.
Father, in your mercy:
forgive us and help us.   *CFW no. 511 adapted* [2]

7   *City, World and Society*

Lord God, our maker and our redeemer,
this is your world and we are your people:
come among us and save us.

We have wilfully misused your gifts of creation,
Lord, be merciful:
forgive us our sin.

We have seen the ill-treatment of others
and have not gone to their aid,
Lord, be merciful:
forgive us our sin.

15

We have condoned evil and dishonesty
and failed to strive for justice,
Lord, be merciful:
forgive us our sin.

We have heard the good news of Christ,
but have failed to share it with others
Lord, be merciful:
forgive us our sin.

We have not loved you with all our heart,
nor our neighbours as ourselves,
Lord, be merciful:
forgive us our sin.   *CFW no. 51 adapted* [2]

8   *Reconciliation*

Let us return to the Lord our God and say to him:

**Father,
we have sinned against heaven and against you.
We are not worthy to be called your children.
We turn to you again.
Have mercy on us,
bring us back to yourself
as those who once were dead
but now have life through Christ our Lord. Amen.**

Luke 15

9   *Love, Peace*

Come let us return to the Lord and say:

**Lord our God,
we have sinned and avoided your call.
Our love for you is like a morning cloud
like the dew that goes away early.
Have mercy on us;
deliver us from judgement;
bind up our wounds
and revive us;
in Jesus Christ our Lord. Amen.**

Hosea 6

10   *General*

God our Father,
we come to you in sorrow for our sins:

For turning away from you,
and ignoring your will for our lives:
Father, forgive us:
save us and help us.

For behaving just as we wish,
without thinking of you:
Father, forgive us:
save us and help us.

For failing you by what we do,
and think and say:
Father, forgive us:
save us, and help us.

For letting ourselves be drawn away from you
by temptations in the world about us:
Father, forgive us:
save us and help us.

For living as if we were ashamed
to belong to your Son:
Father, forgive us:
save us and help us.   *CFW no. 135 adapted* [2]

11   *General*

God our Father,
long-suffering, full of grace and truth.
You create us from nothing and give us life.
You redeem us and make us your children
in the water of baptism.
You do not turn your face from us,
nor cast us aside.
We confess that we have sinned
against you and our neighbour.
We have wounded your love
and marred your image in us.
Restore us for the sake of your Son,

and bring us to heavenly joy,
in Jesus Christ our Lord.   Amen.

12   *General*

Almighty and most merciful Father,
we have wandered and strayed from your ways
      like lost sheep.
We have followed too much the devices and desires
      of our own hearts.
We have offended against your holy laws.
We have left undone those things that we ought
      to have done;
And we have done those things that we ought not
      to have done;
And there is no health in us.
But you, O Lord, have mercy upon us in our need.
Spare those who confess their faults.
Restore those who are penitent,
according to your promises declared to mankind
      in Christ Jesus our Lord.
And grant, O most merciful Father, for his sake,
that from this time we may live a disciplined,
      righteous and godly life,
to the glory of your holy name. Amen.

13   *General*

Almighty God, Father of our Lord Jesus Christ,
      Maker of all things, judge of all people,
We acknowledge and confess
      the grievous sins and wickedness
      which we have so often committed
      by thought, word and deed
      against your divine majesty,
      provoking most justly your anger
      and indignation against us.
We earnestly repent,
      and are deeply sorry for these our wrongdoings;
      the memory of them weighs us down,
      the burden of them is too great for us to bear.

Have mercy upon us,
    have mercy upon us, most merciful Father,
For your Son our Lord Jesus Christ's sake,
    forgive us all that is past;
And grant that from this time onwards
    we may always serve and please you
    in newness of life,
    to the honour and glory of your name,
through Jesus Christ our Lord. Amen.

14   *General*

Man born of woman has but a short time to live. [1]
We have our fill of sorrow.
We blossom like a flower and wither away.
We slip away like a shadow and do not stay.

Holy God,
holy and strong,
holy and immortal,
have mercy upon us.

In the midst of life we are in death;
where can we turn for help?
Only to you, Lord,
who are justly angered by our sins.

Holy God,
holy and strong,
holy and immortal,
have mercy upon us.

Shut not your ears to our prayers,
but spare us, O Lord.

Holy God,
holy and strong,
holy and immortal,
have mercy upon us.

You know the secrets of our hearts;
forgive us our sins.

---

[1] *or* Those born of woman have but a short time to live.

Holy God,
holy and strong,
holy and immortal,
have mercy upon us.

Eternal and merciful judge,
both in life and when we come to die,
let us not fall away from you.

Holy God,
holy and mighty,
holy and merciful Saviour,
do not abandon us to the bitterness of eternal death.

15   *General*

Almighty God,
long-suffering and of great goodness:
I confess to you,
I confess with my whole heart
my neglect and forgetfulness of your commandments,
my wrong doing, thinking, and speaking;
the hurts I have done to others;
and the good I have left undone.
O God, forgive me, for I have sinned against you;
and raise me to newness of life;
through Jesus Christ our Lord. Amen.   3

16   *General*

My God, for love of you
I desire to hate and forsake all sins
by which I have ever displeased you;
and I resolve by the help of your grace
to commit them no more;
and to avoid all opportunities of sin.
Help me to do this,
through Jesus Christ our Lord. Amen.

2   ABSOLUTIONS

1   May almighty God have mercy on us,
    forgive us our sins,
    and bring us to everlasting life,
    through Jesus Christ our Lord. **Amen.**

2   May the God of all healing and forgiveness
    draw us to himself,
    that we may behold the glory of his Son,
    the Word made flesh,
    and be cleansed from all our sins
    through Jesus Christ our Lord. **Amen.**

3   May the Father of all mercies
    cleanse us from our sins,
    and restore us in his service
    to the praise and glory of his name,
    through Jesus Christ our Lord. **Amen.**   *CFW no. 220 adapted* [2]

4   God who is both power and love,
    forgive you and free you from your sins,
    heal and strengthen you by his Spirit,
    and raise you to new life in Christ our Lord. **Amen.**

5   May the Father forgive us
    by the death of his Son
    and strengthen us
    to live in the power of the Spirit
    all our days. Amen.

6   The Lord enrich you with his grace,
    and nourish you with his blessing;
    the Lord defend you in trouble and keep you from all evil;
    the Lord accept your prayers,
    and absolve you from your offences,
    for the sake of Jesus Christ, our Saviour. **Amen.**

7   May God who loved the world so much
    that he sent his Son to be our Saviour
    forgive us our sins
    and make us holy to serve him in the world,
    through Jesus Christ our Lord. **Amen.**

8   May God our Father forgive us our sins,
and bring us to the fellowship of his table
with his saints for ever. **Amen.**

9   May the God of love
bring us back to himself,
forgive us our sins,
and assure us of his eternal love
in Jesus Christ our Lord. **Amen.**

10   Almighty God,
who in Jesus Christ has given us
a kingdom that cannot be destroyed,
forgive us our sins,
open our eyes to God's truth,
strengthen us to do God's will
and give us the joy of his kingdom,
through Jesus Christ our Lord. **Amen.**

11   God, the Father of mercies,
has reconciled the world to himself
through the death and resurrection
of his Son Jesus Christ,
not counting our trespasses against us,
but sending his Holy Spirit
to shed abroad his love among us.
By the ministry of reconciliation
entrusted by Christ to his Church,
receive his pardon and peace
to stand before him in his strength alone,
this day and evermore. **Amen.**

The Promise of His Glory

12   The almighty and merciful Lord
grant you pardon and forgiveness of all your sins,
time for amendment of life,
and the grace and strength of the Holy Spirit. **Amen.**

The Promise of His Glory

13   May Almighty God,
who sent his Son into the world to save sinners,
bring you his pardon and peace, now and for ever. **Amen.**

The Promise of His Glory

AFFIRMATIONS OF FAITH

Notwithstanding the provisions in Rites A or B of ASB 1980, the Apostles' Creed or the Athanasian Creed in an authorized form may be used in place of the Nicene Creed.

The following adaptations of the historic creeds and other Affirmations of Faith may only be used in non-statutory services or in an authorized Service of the Word. On any occasion, suitable words of introduction or conclusion (such as those indicated) to the Creed or Affirmation of Faith may be used.

I

The Nicene Creed may be used responsively as follows:

We believe in one God,
the Father, the almighty:
maker of heaven and earth,
of all that is,
seen and unseen.

We believe in one Lord, Jesus Christ,
the only Son of God,
eternally begotten of the Father:
God from God, Light from Light,
true God from true God,
begotten, not made,
of one Being with the Father:
Through him all things were made.
For us men and for our salvation
he came down from heaven;
by the power of the Holy Spirit
he became incarnate of the Virgin Mary,
and was made man.
For our sake he was crucified under Pontius Pilate;
he suffered death and was buried.
On the third day he rose again
in accordance with the Scriptures:
he ascended into heaven
and is seated at the right hand of the Father.
He will come again in glory
to judge the living and the dead,
and his kingdom will have no end.

We believe in the Holy Spirit:
the Lord, the giver of life,
who proceeds from the Father and the Son:
with the Father and the Son he is worshipped and glorified.
He has spoken through the Prophets.

We believe in one holy, catholic and apostolic Church.
We acknowledge one baptism for the forgiveness of sins:
We look for the resurrection of the dead,
and the life of the world to come. Amen.

II

In addition to the Nicene Creed, the Apostles' Creed and the Athanasian Creed, the following Creeds and Affirmations of Faith are also authorized.

1   Do you believe and trust in God the Father,
who made all things?

We believe and trust in him.

Do you believe and trust in his Son Jesus Christ,
who redeemed the world?

We believe and trust in him.

Do you believe and trust in his Holy Spirit,
who gives life to the people of God?

We believe and trust in him.

This is the faith of the Church:

This is our faith.
We believe and trust in one God,
Father, Son and Holy Spirit. Amen.

2 Do you believe and trust in God the Father,
who made all things?

**I believe in God, the Father almighty,
creator of heaven and earth.**

Do you believe and trust in his Son Jesus Christ,
who redeemed the world?

**I believe in Jesus Christ, his only Son, our Lord.
He was conceived by the power of the Holy Spirit
and born of the Virgin Mary.
He suffered under Pontius Pilate,
was crucified, died, and was buried.
He descended to the dead.
On the third day he rose again.
He ascended into heaven,
and is seated at the right hand of the Father.
He will come again to judge the living and the dead.**

Do you believe and trust in the Holy Spirit,
who gives life to the people of God?

**I believe in the Holy Spirit,
the holy catholic Church,
the communion of saints,
the forgiveness of sins,
the resurrection of the body,
and the life everlasting.**

This is the faith of the Church.

**This is our faith.
We believe and trust in one God,
Father, Son and Holy Spirit.**

3 We proclaim the Church's faith in Jesus Christ:

**We believe and declare that our Lord Jesus Christ,
the Son of God, is both divine and human;**

God, of the being of the Father,
the only Son from before time began;
human from the being of his mother, born in the world.

**Fully God and fully human;
human in both mind and body.**

As God he is equal to the Father,
as human he is less than the Father.

**Although he is both divine and human
he is not two beings but one Christ.**

One, not by turning God into flesh,
but by taking humanity into God.
**Truly one, not by mixing humanity with Godhead,
but by being one person.**

For as mind and body form one human being,
so the one Christ is both divine and human.

**The Word became flesh and lived among us;
we have seen his glory,
the glory of the only Son from the Father,
full of grace and truth.**

from the Athanasian Creed

4   We believe in God the Father,
    God Almighty, by whose plan
    earth and heaven sprang to being,
    all created things began.
    We believe in Christ the Saviour,
    Son of God in human frame,
    virgin-born, the child of Mary
    upon whom the Spirit came.

    Christ, who on the cross forsaken,
    like a lamb to slaughter led,
    suffered under Pontius Pilate,
    he descended to the dead.
    We believe in Jesus risen,
    heaven's king to rule and reign,
    to the Father's side ascended
    till as judge he comes again.

    We believe in God the Spirit;
    in one church, below, above:
    saints of God in one communion,
    one in holiness and love.
    So by faith, our sins forgiven,
    Christ our Saviour, Lord and Friend,
    we shall rise with him in glory
    to the life that knows no end.

copyright Timothy Dudley-Smith [4]

[4] Numbers in right-hand margin refer to Acknowledgements (page 32).

5   Let us affirm our faith in Jesus Christ the Son of God:

Though he was divine,
he did not cling to equality with God,
but made himself nothing.
Taking the form of a slave,
he was born in human likeness.
He humbled himself,
and was obedient to death -
even the death of the cross.
Therefore God has raised him on high,
and given him the name above every name:
that at the name of Jesus
every knee should bow,
and every voice proclaim that Jesus Christ is Lord,
to the glory of God the Father. Amen.

Philippians 2.9-11
CFW *no. 212 adapted* [2]

6   Let us declare our faith
in the resurrection of our Lord Jesus Christ:

Christ died for our sins
in accordance with the scriptures;
he was buried;
he was raised to life on the third day
in accordance with the scriptures;
afterwards he appeared to his followers,
and to all the apostles:
this we have received,
and this we believe. Amen.   *1 Corinthians 15.3-7*
CFW *no. 256* [2]

7 We say together in faith:

Holy, holy, holy
is the Lord God Almighty,
who was, and is, and is to come.

We believe in God the Father,
who created all things:

for by his will they were created
and have their being.

We believe in God the Son,
who was slain:

for with his blood,
he purchased us for God,
from every tribe and language,
from every people and nation.

We believe in God the Holy Spirit –

the Spirit and the Bride say, 'Come!'
Even so, come Lord Jesus! Amen.   *Revelation 4.8,11; 5.9; 22.17*
                                               CFW no. 591 adapted [2]

8 Let us declare our faith in God:

We believe in God the Father,
from whom every family
in heaven and on earth is named.
We believe in God the Son,
who lives in our hearts through faith,
and fills us with his love.

We believe in God the Holy Spirit,
who strengthens us
**   with power from on high.**

We believe in one God;
Father, Son, and Holy Spirit. Amen.   *From Ephesians 3*
                                              CFW no. 192 [2]

This **Affirmation of Commitment** may be used after
an authorized Creed or Affirmation of Faith:

Will you continue in the apostles' teaching and
fellowship, in the breaking of bread,
and in the prayers?

With the help of God, I will.

Will you persevere in resisting evil, and,
whenever you fall into sin, repent and return to the Lord?

With the help of God, I will.

Will you proclaim by word and example
the good news of God in Christ?

With the help of God, I will.

Will you seek and serve Christ in all people,
loving your neighbour as yourself?

With the help of God, I will.

Will you acknowledge Christ's authority over human society,
by prayer for the world and its leaders,
by defending the weak, and by seeking peace and justice?

With the help of God, I will.   5

ACKNOWLEDGEMENTS

Thanks are due to those whose names are listed below, for permission to include copyright texts in *A Service of the Word* and *Affirmations of Faith*. The number which precedes each acknowledgement is used in the text to indicate the material to which the permission relates. The numbers appear in the right hand margin.

2   [Texts originally published in *Church Family Worship (CFW)*]
     The Reverend Michael Perry; copyright administered by
     Jubilate Hymns Ltd.

3   The Society for Promoting Christian Knowledge: Eric Milner-
     White, *My God my Glory*, definitive edition 1967; as adapted by
     David Silk for *In Penitence and Faith*, Mowbray 1988.

4   The Rt Revd Timothy Dudley-Smith
     copyright Timothy Dudley-Smith

     (May be sung to any 87 87 or 87 87D tune. Recommended
     tunes are Lux Eoi (Arthur Sullivan), Alleluia (S S Wesley),
     Abbot's Leigh (Cyril Taylor). Churches in membership of the
     Christian Copyright Licensing scheme should record use on
     their return.)

5   The Anglican Church of Canada

The arrangements for *local editions* as defined in *Liturgical Texts for Local Use* (see page 2) cover the inclusion of these copyright texts provided that the individual copyrights are acknowledged as indicated above. In all other cases application should be made to the copyright owner or administrator or to the Central Board of Finance.